Contents

Introduction

Living things include the plants, animals, *fungi* and algae that we can see, as well as the tiny organisms such as *bacteria* and protozoa which can be seen only with a microscope. These organisms live in every type of habitat on Earth – on land and in lakes, rivers and seas. Some organisms, such as some worms, bacteria and protozoa, live in both water and soil.

Arctic lupin

The record for the world's oldest germinated seed is an arctic lupin (lupinus arcticus). Found in a lemming burrow in frozen Arctic tundra, the seed actually germinated and flowered after an estimated 10.000 years!

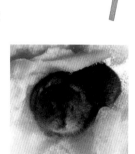

Lemming in burrow

Rafflesia flower

Scientists think that there are over a million species of fungi in the world, but only about 10 per cent have been properly described.

Fungus

The rainforests of Borneo are home to the world's biggest flower, called the rafflesia. It's a parasitic plant with no stem or leaves, but with roots buried in the tissue of its host vine. It needs flies to spread its pollen to other flowers, so it attracts them by producing the smell of rotting meat!

Man belongs to a group of animals called mammals. Also in the group are possibly the smallest, the Kitti's hog-nosed bat, from Thailand, weighing only about 2 gm and around 12 mm long, fully grown. The largest is generally agreed to be the blue whale, weighing sometimes up to 170,000 kg and around 33 m long!

Blue whale

Kitti's hog-nosed bat   Algae

Algae used to be considered no more than primitive plants, but are now seen as an essential and complex part of the life on our world. Algae have *chlorophyll*, like plants, and manufacture their own food from nutrients and sunlight.

Another record for survival is the Asian water lotus (Nelumbo nucifera). A seed from China was grown after 1,200 years.

Asian water lotus

Bacteria have a very simple form of life, but they can really thrive in the environment to which they are adapted.

Bacteria grown in the laboratory

Friends can help...
Do the experiments with your friends!

Jargon Buster

A **mammal** is an animal that has a backbone, hair or fur and gives birth to live young which it feeds with milk.

Some technical or unusual words, shown in *italic* type, are explained in the glossary on page 31.

Materials and tools

You should easily find many things that you need for our experiments around the home.

20 minutes

This tells you about how long a project could take.

This symbol means you might need adult help.

Tape We use sticky tape to hold things in position. Masking tape or clear parcel tape will do.

Waterproof tape When we need

to make stronger joins, it's best to use thicker, waterproof tape sometimes called 'duct tape'.

Glue stick is mostly used for sticking paper to paper. Universal glue is a rubbery stuff that sticks most things to most other things!

Scissors Ask an adult for an old pair of scissors that you can keep for all your experiments. They will be very useful. Keep them away from young children.

Plastic dropper Available from art and craft shops. Ideal for controlling drops of liquid.

String Ordinary household string will be fine for most of our needs.

Funnel Very useful for filtering liquids when used with filter paper or kitchen roll. Also handy when filling bottles. We also use funnels with sound! See page 26.

Tubes Collect cardboard tubes from kitchen towels or other paper rolls to use in experiments.

Food dye Small bottles of food dye are available from supermarkets for colouring cakes and sweets. It's very strong. You will only need a few drops. Avoid getting dye on your clothes!

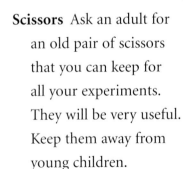

Plastic bottles Ask an adult for empty plastic bottles. The ones used for water and soft drinks are best.

Ice lolly sticks These are ideal for stirring mixtures or lighting night lights. Collect them next time you eat ice lollies!

Jam jars Try to save as many different clean, empty jars at home as you can. We are going to need quite a few for the experiments. Afterwards you can recycle them.

Kitchen supplies Be careful when using food ingredients or anything from unmarked bottles. Check with an adult and get permission first.

Notebook Keep a special notebook to record the results of your experiments.

Shoe box Every time someone has new shoes, there might be a box available. Save them for your experiments. Tissue boxes can also be handy. See page 16.

Watering Can See if you can find a small watering can in the garden. It would be ideal to keep your seeds and seedlings carefully watered.

Kitchen roll Paper towels on a roll, very useful for cleaning up and required for quite a few of our experiments.

What do seeds need to grow?

Many plants spread themselves by *scattering* seeds. A seed contains a new plant and enough food for it to start growing.

preparation 20 minutes

You will need:

- paper towel
- thick cardboard
- 4 clean, shallow food trays
- quick-germinating seeds, such as cress
- water

The plan

We are going to find out what else a seed needs to germinate – water, light, warmth? You'll need to collect some food trays for this project.

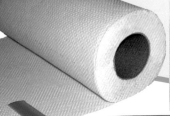

What to do:

1 Put three or four thicknesses of paper towel in the bottom of each tray. Scatter the same number of seeds in each tray. Label them A, B, C, D. Wet the paper towels in trays A, B and C.

A has everything	B no warmth no light	C no light	D no water

2 Put trays A and D near a window in a warm room.

3 Cover tray C with thick cardboard to keep the light out and put it with A and D.

4 Put tray B in the fridge, to give no warmth.

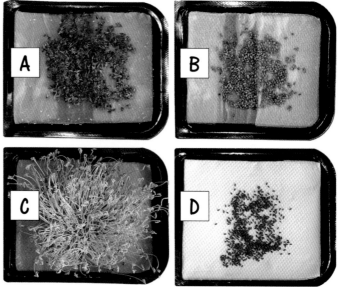

5 Check the trays daily. After five days the seeds should look quite different. (see What's going on?)

What's going on?

Seeds won't germinate without water, but they don't need light. Without warmth, they grow more slowly or don't germinate at all.

What else can you do?

Keep the germinated seedlings in the same conditions and see if their needs are the same.

Plants and gravity

Have you ever wondered why, when you plant seeds, the roots always go down into the soil and the leaves up into the air?

preparation 25 minutes

You will need:

- 4 jam jars, broad bean seeds
- some paper towels or blotting paper
- scissors, water

The plan

We're going to germinate some seeds in different positions to see which way the roots go.

Start with four bean seeds from the packet.

What to do:

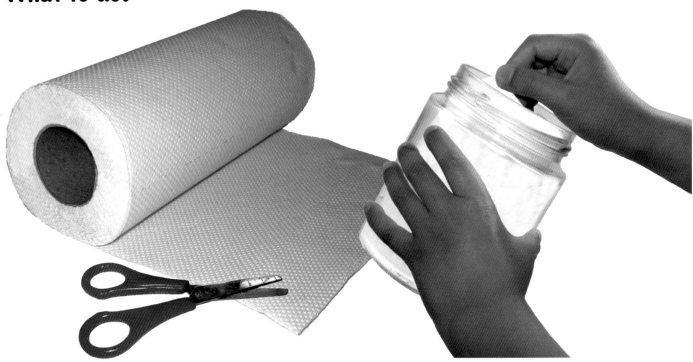

1 Cut a piece of paper towel or blotting paper to fit round the sides of the jar – so that it fits snugly against the sides.

Jargon Buster
Germinate means begin to grow and put out shoots.

The black scar where the bean was attached to its pod.

2 Find the black scar on each seed. Put one seed in each jar, between the glass and the blotting paper.

Make each bean lie in a different direction. The first with the scar up; the second with it down; the third with it to the left; the fourth to the right.

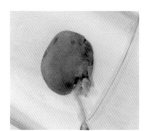

3 Put about 25 mm (1 in) of water in each jar. It should soak into the paper to reach the seeds. Keep the water at this level.

What's going on?

The roots and the shoots always grow from the same point on the seed, but they react to gravity. Roots grow with gravity; shoots grow against gravity.

What else can you do?

After they have germinated, turn the seeds so that the roots are pointing upwards and see what happens.

Transpiration

Plants get their water from the soil, but where does it go from there?

You will need:

- freshly cut white flowers, carnations are ideal
- glass of water, plastic dropper
- food dye, scissors
- *magnifying glass*

The plan

We are going to see where water goes in plants by using dye to follow its path.

What to do:

1 Drop some food dye into a glass of water.

2 Trim the flower stem before putting the flower into the water. Watch as the flower changes colour.

Giant redwood trees in America

3 You should get results something like this!

What's going on?

Plant stems are made up of long hollow cells like a series of drinking straws. As water *evaporates* from the leaves, water is drawn up the plant from the soil. This occurs

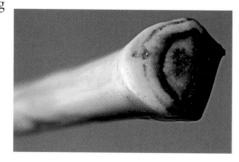

in all plants. Giant redwood trees grow to over 100 m (350 ft) and draw water up their trunks in this way.

What else can you do?

Try dyeing coloured flowers and see what new colours you get, test a red flower and green dye.

Use a magnifying glass to examine flower stems to check out the details close up!

Jargon Buster
Transpiration means evaporation from leaves drawing water into a plant.

What do plants prefer?

Have you ever wondered if plants have a *preference* for what they grow in? By testing with *seedlings*, we try to find out when they do best.

45 minutes

You will need:

- 4 same-size seedlings
- 4 similar containers
- *compost*, sand, gravel, soil
- water, labels, pen, notebook

The plan

We are going to see how seedlings develop when planted in different types of growing material.

What to do:

1 Put compost, sand, gravel and garden soil into similar sized containers. We have used clean jam jars.

2 *Transplant* four seedlings from their pots to the containers. Keep in *identical* conditions with light and warmth. Give each plant half a cup of water. Label each jar.

compost

sand

gravel

soil

3 After a week you should be able to see clearly which plants are *thriving* or failing. Do you know why?

4 Remove the BEST plant from the jar to check the root structure. Notice that both the leaves and the roots are *developing* well. This plant **likes** the conditions you have provided.

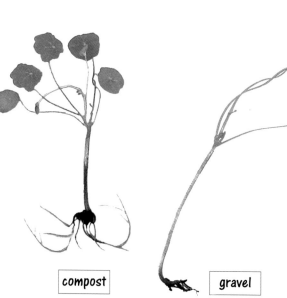

compost

gravel

5 Remove the WORST plant from the jar to check the root structure. The plant is weak. Notice that both the leaves and the roots are not developing well. This plant **does not like** the conditions you have provided.

What's going on?

Results should prove that plants prefer a mixed material to grow in, such as garden soil or compost. Some compost can be too rich, sand can hold too much water and gravel provides no *nutrients*.

What else can you do?

After you have finished observing the plants, find a good place for the healthy ones in a garden so that they have a chance to flourish.

Woodlouse house

You probably have a house that's dry, warm and light – but but would that suit other animals?

The plan

We are going to find out what sort of conditions woodlice like to live in!

You will need:

- 5 cardboard boxes (approximately the same size and shape, such as tissue boxes)
- 4 cardboard tubes, 2 plastic carrier bags
- 2 pieces of cardboard, plastic cling film
- paper towels, sticky tape, marker pen
- At least 15 live woodlice, (look under stones)
- scissors, water, notebook, map pin

What to do:

1 Place a cardboard tube on the long side of a tissue box. Draw round the tube with a marker pen.

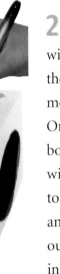

2 Cut out the circle with scissors. Repeat the process on three more boxes. On the last box you will need to mark and cut out a hole in each side.

3 Cut out the top of all five boxes, leaving a 10 mm (0.4 in) border around the edge. Mark the boxes A, B, C, D and E.

4 Line the bases of all the boxes inside with plastic sheet cut from a carrier bag, then put in two layers of paper towel. Dampen the paper in boxes A and B.

5 Stretch plastic cling film over two of the boxes, A and C. Use thick card, cut to the right size, to cover two more boxes, B and D. Use tape to fix the covers.

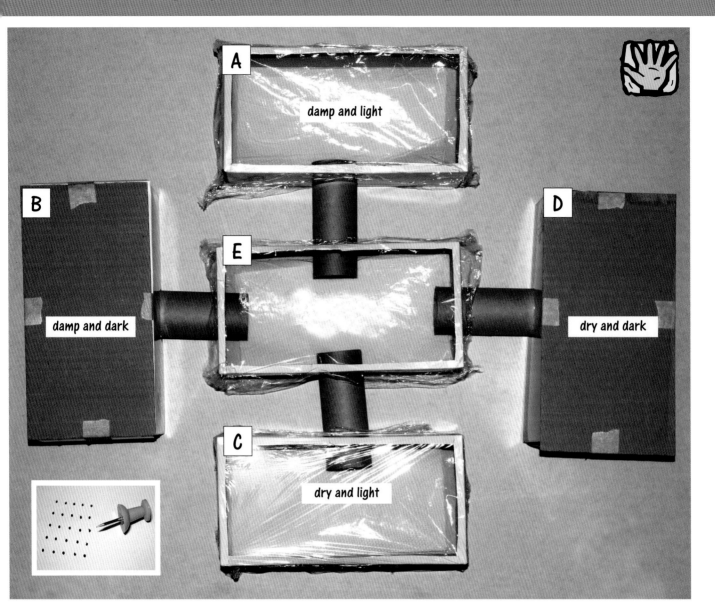

A
damp and light

B
damp and dark

D
dry and dark

E

C
dry and light

6 Push the tubes into each box and connect them up as shown in the photograph above. Fix the tubes with tape. Make pin holes in the sides of all boxes for air (see inset picture above).

7 Place the woodlice in box E, cover box with cling film. Over a period of four days, carefully check the numbers of woodlice in each outer box to see which one they prefer! Make notes of results.

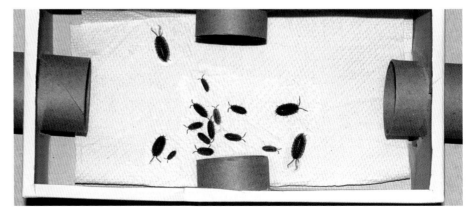

What's going on?

Like plants, animals are adapted to different living conditions – what suits one could be *fatal* to another.

Very Important!

Put the woodlice back where you found them once you have finished *observing* them!

A wormery

60 minutes

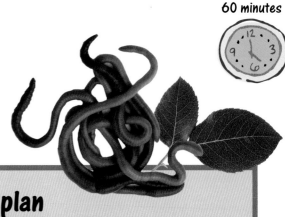

We know that worms live under the ground. What do they do there? And why are they popular with gardeners?

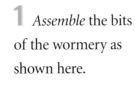

You will need:

- 2 sheets of clear plastic about 300 mm (12 in) square
- 3 pieces of wood 25 x 50 mm (1 x 2 in) cut as follows: 1 piece 300 mm (12 in), 2 pieces 275mm (11 in)
- strong waterproof tape
- universal glue, scissors
- sand, soil, leaves, grass and earthworms

The plan

We are going to make a wormery that allows us to see what is going on underground.

What to do:

1 *Assemble* the bits of the wormery as shown here.

2 Lay one sheet of plastic on a table, put the longest piece of wood at the base. Fix with universal glue. Add the two sides.

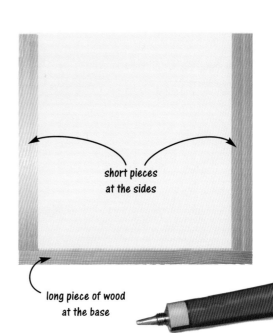

short pieces at the sides

long piece of wood at the base

Jargon Buster
Lumbricus terrestris is the scientific name for the earthworm.

3 Allow the glue to dry completely. Spread more glue on the surface of wooden frame to fix the second piece of plastic. This completes the box. But you could tape all round the frame for extra *stability*.

4 Add soil and sand in 25 mm (1 in) layers. Dampen the sand with water. Put the worms on the top layer. Add some leaves and bits of grass for food. Keep the soil damp and do not over-water.

5 Observe the wormery over several days and weeks. Make notes about the results.

worms move the layers around

worms drag the leaves underground

soil
sand
soil
sand
soil
sand
soil
sand

What's going on?

The worms mix up the soil as they move about and feed. They also break up lumps of soil and dry leaves, which become food for plants. Their *burrows* allow air into the soil, which also helps break down plant material. All these activities improve the soil, so most gardeners like worms in their garden.

What else can you do?

Put tiny pieces of grated vegetables on the top layer to check if your worms like a varied diet!

Very important!

When your experiment is finished, return your worms to the place you found them.

Microorganisms

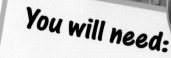

Microorganisms (bacteria, fungi, *viruses* etc) are much more numerous than we are. Some are harmful, carrying disease, whilst others are useful, for example, in bread making and for fighting disease.

The plan

We are going to try growing microorganisms in different conditions.

You will need:

- 4 slices of bread
- 4 plastic bags
- sticky tape
- marker pen
- water
- magnifying glass

What to do:

1 Put three slices of bread into three separate plastic bags marked A, B and C. Seal the ends with tape.

2 Dampen the fourth slice of bread with water and put it into the plastic bag marked D. Seal with more tape.

A
no light

B
no light
no warmth

3 Put bag A into a dark place, such as a cupboard.

4 Put bag B into a fridge.

C
warm and
light

D
warm, light
and damp

5 Put bag C and bag D into the same warm, light place. Examine all the bags daily (DO NOT OPEN THE BAGS).

6 Record amount and colour of mould in a notebook. Check the mould through the plastic with magnifying glass.

What's going on?

Moulds are a type of fungus. All fungi like warm, dark places. As we have been learning, living things are adapted for a wide range of conditions.

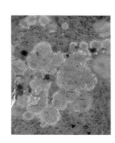

What else can you do?

See the next page for more experiments to find out where microorganisms will grow!

WARNING!

Do not breath in spores. Wash your hands often.

More microorganisms

20 minutes

You will need:

- empty plastic water bottle
- sticky tape
- 4 jars of water
- string and 4 sticks
- hole punch
- scissors, teaspoon
- plasticine, 4 lolly sticks
- foods – jam, marmalade, tomato sauce and mustard or similar
  (DO NOT USE ANIMAL PRODUCTS)

The plan

We're going to find out what happens with different foods in water.

What to do:

1 Cut four strips of plastic from an empty water bottle. Make each 25 x 75 mm (1 x 3 in).

2 Make a small hole at the end of each strip with a hole punch. Tie a 100 mm (6 in) string to each strip.

22

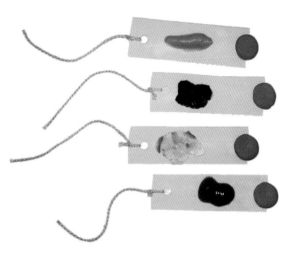

3 Add a lump of plasticine on each strip as a weight.

4 Spread half a teaspoonful of one food on each strip.

| jam | mustard | tomato sauce | marmalade |

5 Fill the jars with water. Carefully lower each strip into the water. Tie the string to a lolly stick.

6 Observe what happens to the food samples each day for a week. Keep notes in your notebook.

What's going on?

Some microorganisms are adapted to live in water. Check samples with a magnifying glass, through the jar. Note which food gets attacked first.

Warning!

Dispose of all samples and jars safely after use. Wash your hands frequently. Avoid contamination with other food.

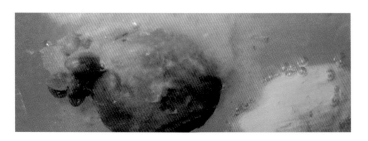

Jargon Buster
Contamination means spoiling something by adding another material to it.

23

Sight

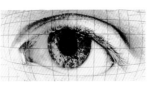

So far we have experimented with some of the living things in the world around us. But we are alive, too, and we can also experiment on ourselves!

You will need:

- small table
- large sheet of paper for the *target*
- 3 different coloured thick-tip marker pens, a tin lid
- scissors and thin card for the spinner
- pencil, glue stick
- string

The plan

We are going to learn a bit about how our eyes work and how using two eyes is often better than one!

Experiment 1

1 Draw your target on paper and put it flat on a table.

2

  Cover one eye.
To test your aim, hold a marker pen with the top removed, at arm's length. Try to drop it on the centre of the target.

  Cover the other eye.
Repeat the test and try to hit the target with next marker.

 Use both eyes.
Repeat test with the last pen.

Experiment 2

1 Draw round a tin lid with a marker. Cut out two discs from your card to make a spinner.

2 Draw a simple bird cage on one disc and a black bird on the other one. Stick the discs together, back to back, with one drawing upside-down.

3 Make a hole on each side of the card and tie a string to each hole. Holding the strings, flip the circle of card so that the strings twist over and over.

4 Pull the strings tight so that the disc spins back and forth quickly. As you watch you will see the two drawings combine – now the bird is in the cage!

What's going on?

In Experiment 1 – are some marks off target? Each eye sees things from a slightly different angle. The brain compares the two different images and works out how far away objects are. With only one eye it cannot do this.

In Experiment 2 – an image of what we see remains on the retina of the eye for a fraction of a second after the object disappears. Because the movement of the card is so rapid, the image is still there when it has spun round, so we see both sides of the card at once.

Jargon Buster

Stereoscopic vision is possible thanks to the close side-by-side positioning of our eyes. Each sees the same area from a slightly different angle. The eye views have plenty in common, but each eye picks up visual information the other doesn't.

Hearing

The sense of hearing has qualities that we often take for granted. Here's an experiment that shows how our ears help us find our way around.

Get friends to help you!

You will need:

- a friend to be the 'subject'
- 5 m (12 ft) of plastic hosepipe
- 2 plastic *funnels*
- blindfold
- notebook, pen or pencil
- 4 more friends

The plan

We're going to see how well we can tell the direction a noise is coming from, without relying on our eyes.

What to do:

1 Cut the hosepipe in half. Push a funnel into each hose.

2 Get a friend or classmate to stand in an open space. Put a blindfold around his or her eyes. They now become 'Subject A' for your hearing experiment! Position the other people around them, without letting the subject know where they are.

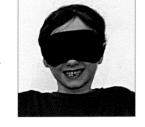

3 In turn, each person claps their hands together once. After each clap the subject must point in the direction of the noise. Do they guess ✓ right or ✗ not?

Clap!
Clap!
Clap!
Clap!
Clap!

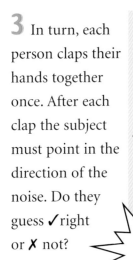

Subject A		Subject B	
1	✓	1	✗
2	✓	2	✓
3	✗	3	✓
4	✓	4	✗
5	✗	5	✗

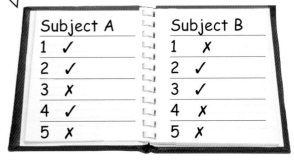

4 Write down the results in your notebook to compare with the answers in the next part.

5 Keep the subject blindfolded. He or she becomes 'Subject B'. Ask the subject to hold the ends of both the hosepipes to their ears. Get two people to hold a funnel each and point it in random directions.

6 Repeat Step 3, but this time the subject must turn to face the direction they think the noise is coming from. Record the answers in your notebook.

7 Compare your results for Step 3 and Step 6. What difference do the hosepipes and funnels make to the answers?

What's going on?

Just as we have stereoscopic vision, we also have stereophonic hearing, which in a similar way helps us to identify the direction from which a sound is coming.

What else can you do?

Test how easy it is to find the direction of a sound with only one ear. Put a hand over the other ear. Then get a friend to help you find the direction of the sound with the hose and funnel!

Jargon Buster
Subject means the person selected to be the main part of the experiment.

Touch

Touch is another important sense we rely on to keep us safe. It lets us experience sensations like hot and cold, rough and smooth, wet and dry, soft and hard.

The plan

To see if your friends can identify hidden objects by feel and touch alone.

What to do:

1 Cut two holes in the sides of the cardboard box, big enough to get your fist through. Decorate the box with coloured shapes or marker pens.

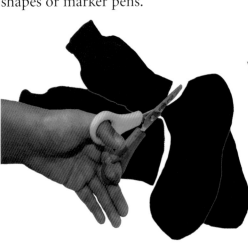

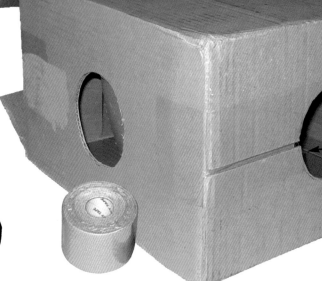

Use the tape inside the box to fix sock 'sleeve'.

2 Cut the straight bits off two old black socks (ask before you ruin dad's best footwear). Use strong tape to fix them on the inside of the box, so they make 'sleeves' coming out of the box. Put your hands through the socks to feel the objects in the box without seeing them.

Experiment 1

1 Things to try in the box: spoon, tennis ball, toys, fruit, pencil, cotton reel, pine cone, sunglasses, slipper, brush, tin foil, keys, oven glove, empty match box and so on.

2 Put several things in the box at the same time, without anyone else seeing. You can either have two people playing using one hand each, or one person using both hands.

3 Ask how many items are in the box . To help them guess an object ask questions: 'Is it heavy?' 'Is it light?' Discuss the texture of objects: smooth, rough, bumpy, soft, hard and so on. *Record* results to see who gets the most right.

Experiment 2

Wearing a pair of washing up gloves, each person has another go using different objects. Again, everyone tries to guess what is in the box this time. Compare the results with Experiment 1.

What's going on?

You can now judge what happens when you reduce the amount of tactile (touch) information getting to your brain. Just relying on what you can feel can be really tricky!

Taste and smell

Seventy to seventy-five per cent of what we think is taste actually comes from our sense of smell. Taste buds allow us to recognise only a few flavours. It's the odour molecules from food that give us most of our taste sensations!

You will need:

- 4 different flavours of potato crisps
- blindfold
- notebook and pencil
- some willing friends

The plan

We're going to see how well people can tell which foods they're eating by only relying on the senses of taste or smell.

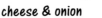
A
cheese & onion

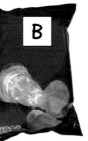
B
salt & vinegar

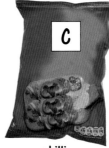
C
chilli

D
prawn

What to do:

1 Blindfold the first volunteer. Ask him or her to pinch their nose while they taste each item.

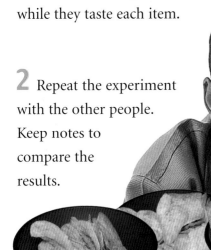

2 Repeat the experiment with the other people. Keep notes to compare the results.

A   B   C   D

What's going on?

We really can only taste four things: bitter, salty, sweet and sour. Much of what we think we taste, we actually smell!

Jargon Buster

A **molecule** is the smallest particle into which a substance can be divided without chemical change. **Odour molecules** produce particular smells.

Glossary

Animal products   Foods which come from animals, such as meat, eggs, butter, milk and cheese.

Approximately   Fairly accurately but not totally precisely.

Assemble   Arrange in an ordered way; put items together correctly.

Bacteria   A large group of single cell microorganisms, some of which cause diseases.

Burrows   Holes or tunnels dug by small animals making a home.

Chlorophyll   Chemical that green plants use to help make their food.

Compost   Decayed organic material used as a fertiliser for growing plants.

Developing   Growing and becoming larger or more advanced.

Evaporates   Turns from a liquid into a vapour.

Fatal   Causing death to a plant or animal.

Fungi   Plural of 'fungus', spore-producing organisms which feed on organic matter.

Funnel   Cone-shaped item used to assist with pouring liquids into narrow bottles.

Gravity   The force which attracts things towards the centre of the Earth.

Identical   Exactly alike, the same as.

Nutrients   Substances that provide food needed for life and growth.

Magnifying   Making something larger than it is, in this case with the use of a lens.

Observing   Watching something very carefully.

Preference   A greater liking for one alternative over another or others.

Record   To make an accurate note of and keep for future reference.

Scattering   Throwing in various random directions.

Seedlings   Seeds which have just sprouted leaves and roots, becoming small plants.

Stability   In this case, rigidity and holding together securely.

Target   A round board with concentric rings to be aimed at.

Transplant   Move to a another place or situation or replant a plant.

Thriving   Doing well, developing correctly.

Viruses   Sub-microscopic particles causing infection by multiplying cells.

Index

Websites

http://www.abc.net.au/spark/experiments/list.htm
http://pbskids.org/zoom/activities/sci/
http://sciencemadesimple.com/
http://wow.osu.edu/experiments.php